Let's Draw
Animals

Author
Susie Hodge

Artist
Steve Roberts

WINDMILL
BOOKS

New York

Published in 2011 by Windmill Books, LLC
303 Park Avenue South, Suite #1280, New York, NY 10010-3657

Adaptations to North American Edition © 2011 Windmill Books, LLC
Copyright © 2011 Miles Kelly Publishing

Library of Congress Cataloging-in-Publication Data

Hodge, Susie, 1960–
Animals / by Susie Hodge ; illustrated by Steve Roberts.
p. cm. — (Let's draw)
Includes index.
ISBN 978-1-61533-269-4 (library binding) —
ISBN 978-1-61533-270-0 (pbk.) — ISBN 978-1-61533-292-2 (6-pack)
1. Animals in art—Juvenile literature. 2. Drawing—Technique—Juvenile
literature. I. Roberts, Steve. II. Title.
NC780.H56 2011
743.6—dc22

2010042195

Manufactured in the United States of America

CPSIA Compliance Information: Batch #BW2011WM: For Further Information contact Windmill Books,
New York, New York at 1-866-478-0556

R0425983146

contents

Materials _____ 4

Shading _____ 6

Texture _____ 8

Perspective _____ 10

Action _____ 11

Penguin _____ 12

Frog _____ 14

Shark _____ 16

Bear _____ 18

Dog _____ 20

Parrot _____ 22

Lion _____ 24

Giraffe _____ 26

Horse _____ 28

Cat _____ 30

Read More _____ 32

Glossary _____ 32

Index _____ 32

Web Sites _____ 32

Materials

ALL YOU NEED TO START DRAWING IS A PENCIL AND SOME PAPER. IF YOU COLLECT SOME OTHER MATERIALS, THOUGH, YOU WILL BE ABLE TO CREATE EVEN MORE EXCITING EFFECTS IN YOUR DRAWINGS.

Pencils

Soft pencils make black, smudgy lines. Hard pencils make light, thin lines.

Soft pencil

Hard pencil

Paper

Try using different types of paper, such as heavy drawing paper, tissue paper, and constuction paper, to add extra texture to your drawings.

Buy handmade paper from gift or art stores.

Textured paper makes an excellent background.

Colored pencils

The simplest way to add color is with colored pencils. Some can be blended with water to turn them into watercolors. You can also layer colored pencils on top of each other to make new colors.

Corrugated paper adds extra depth to bumpy textures.

Charcoal and chalk

Charcoal comes in black, brittle sticks. These can be smudged and blended easily to create shadowy, dramatic pictures. Chalk pastels are good for adding highlights, and are best used on colored paper.

Other equipment

Firm erasers will get rid of most pencil and some colored pencil marks. Kneaded erasers can be squashed into all sorts of shapes to "lift" marks off the page. A good pencil sharpener is useful. Paintbrushes can be used to add water to water-soluble colored pencils.

Felt-tip pens

Pens can be used to add a more cartoonish feel to your drawings. You can use them to define outlines and create dramatic patterns and markings.

Crayons

Wax crayons can be used on their own or with other materials to produce lots of interesting results.

Shading

To help make your animal look more solid and three-dimensional, you need to add shading, or tone, to your drawing.

Light and dark

When light shines on something, the parts nearest the light are palest and the parts farthest from the light are darkest. Try to be aware of where the light is falling on whatever you are drawing.

When the light source is below the dog, its front is palest.

When the light source is above the dog, its back is palest.

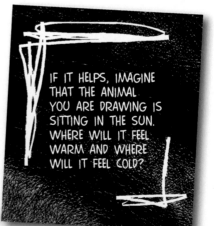

IF IT HELPS, IMAGINE THAT THE ANIMAL YOU ARE DRAWING IS SITTING IN THE SUN. WHERE WILL IT FEEL WARM AND WHERE WILL IT FEEL COLD?

How to shade

A shadow always falls in the opposite direction from the source of light. To make your tones darker, add several layers of pencil or charcoal, or use layers of dark colors to build up depth.

Hatching
Using diagonal lines to shade is called hatching. Draw the lines close together for darker areas and farther apart for lighter areas.

Cross-hatching
For deep shadows, add lines across your hatching in the opposite direction. This makes a crisscross pattern.

Stippling
Create shading using lots of tiny dots.

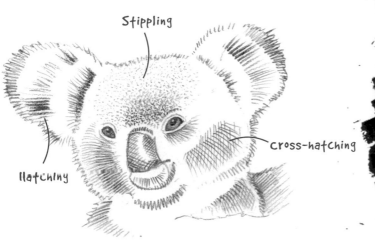

Stippling

Cross-hatching

Hatching

Try it!
Different ways of shading create different effects. Choose which type suits your animal.

Highlights
The opposite of shade is highlight. This is where the light directly falls, so it's the palest area. Sharp and strongly contrasting highlights can make things look shiny. To make highlights, leave areas of white paper blank, add white pastel or colored pencil, or "lift" marks using a kneaded eraser.

Texture

HERE ARE SOME EXAMPLES OF HOW TO MAKE A DRAWING OF AN ANIMAL LOOK THE WAY IT FEELS.

Look and feel

When drawing fur or feathers, start your pencil mark at the base of the hair or feather. Press firmly and lift your pencil as you move to the end of the line.

Feathers
Use long, delicate strokes filled with shorter, soft ones.

Smooth skin
Make the dark areas very dark and the light areas very light.

Fur
Draw lots of short lines going in the same direction.

Bumpy skin
Draw lines, squares, and circles, pressing hard with your pencil.

Patterns and markings

When you are drawing patterns and markings on an animal, try to simplify what you see. Draw simple patterns such as dashes, zigzags, and "U" and "V" shapes.

Patterned skin
Shade carefully in darker areas, leaving light areas pale.

Wrinkly skin
Use short crisscrossing lines. The lines should be darker in dark areas and fade away in the light.

NEVER TRY TO DRAW ALL THE TEXTURES YOU SEE, OR YOUR PICTURE WILL LOOK FLAT. DRAWING LESS TEXTURE IN THE LIGHT PARTS AND MORE IN THE DARKER AREAS HELPS TO SHOW THE ANIMAL'S SHAPE.

perspective

OBJECTS THAT ARE FAR AWAY FROM YOU LOOK SMALL, WHILE OBJECTS THAT ARE VERY CLOSE TO YOU LOOK LARGE. SO IF YOU LOOK AT A DOG FROM THE FRONT, ITS NOSE WILL APPEAR MUCH LARGER THAN ITS TAIL.

Big or small

If you are drawing an animal running toward you, its front feet will look bigger than its back feet. From another angle, one ear might seem bigger than the other, or legs that are farther away may seem much smaller than legs that are closer to you.

Side view
From the side, most animals seem to be in proportion.

Front view
The tail of this shark appears tiny because it is far away. The mouth and nostrils seem huge because they are close.

Action

AS WELL AS DRAWING ANIMALS STANDING STILL OR SITTING, YOU'LL NEED TO PUT THEM IN MOTION.

Flying owl
This owl is about to swoop, so its wings are outstretched.

Get moving!
Decide which direction your animal is moving. Then sweep your pencil quickly across a piece of paper in the same direction. Use that guideline as the basis for your animal.

Once you have drawn the animal, try smudging chalk pastels or draw broken lines to give the idea of movement.

Running horse
The streaming mane and tail show how fast the horse is moving. The head and neck are extended as the horse lunges forward.

Three legs are off the ground at the same time.

penguin

1 Draw a long oval for the body and a small oval for the head. Add a triangle for the tail feathers.

2 Add two curved lines to join the head to the body. Draw the legs and feet using short lines.

3 Draw the eye as a small circle. Add a narrow, curving beak. Add shape to the wing.

Erase this line.

Wobbly line for the edge of the wing

Little lines indicate soft feathers.

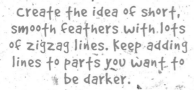

Create the idea of short, smooth feathers with lots of zigzag lines. Keep adding lines to parts you want to be darker.

5 Add areas of orange-yellow around the neck and pale blue to highlight the front.

Patches of dark blue make these feathers look shiny.

4 Shape the toes and claws. Shade in the dark feathers on the back, head, tail, and wing.

The underside of the head and neck is darker.

Add shading to the back leg.

13

Frog

1 Draw a large, sloping oval with a narrow tip. Draw a squashed oval near the bottom for the front leg. Shape the back leg.

Add a bump for this eye.

only part of the back leg can be seen.

This eye is a circle with a curvy line above it.

2 Add the front legs and more detail to the back legs. Shape the head and features.

This line adds shape to the body.

Add a line for the wide mouth.

The back leg forms an "S" shape.

3 Shape the feet and add detail to the head.

only two toes are visible on this foot.

The feet have four long toes.

Try working on textured paper to create bumpy skin. Add color in a circular motion using blunt pencils. Don't press too hard.

4 Color your frog using a mixture of greens and browns to create bumpy-looking skin.

Make rough shapes of different sizes.

Add shadow.

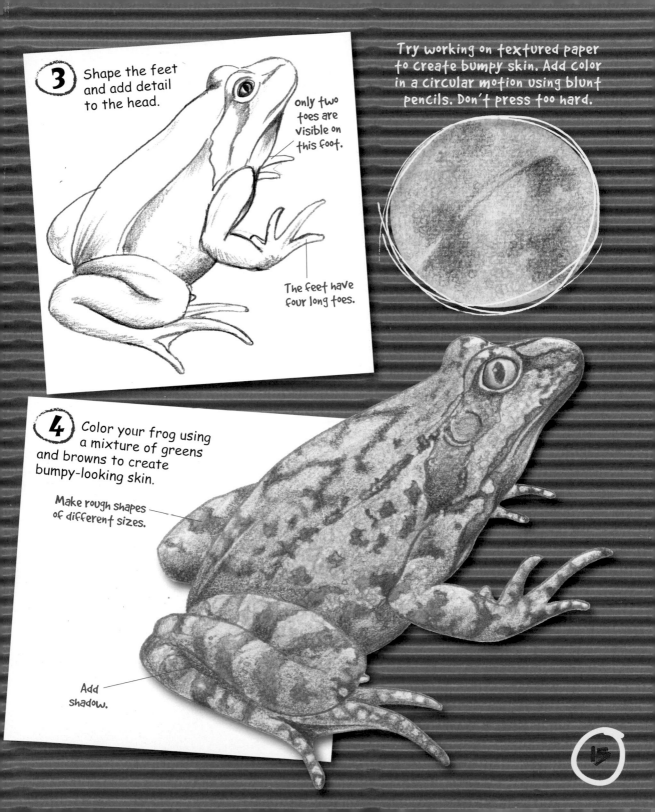

shark

1 Draw the outline and fins using triangular shapes.

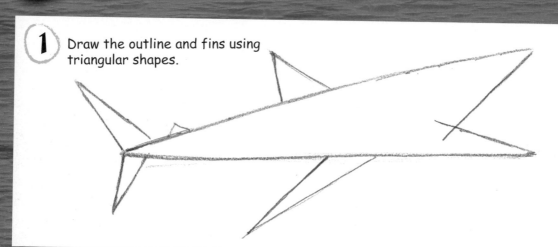

2 Soften your lines, adding shape to the fins.

Add the eye.

Start to add the detail of the markings on the skin.

Try coloring your shark with watercolor pencils. Then wet a soft brush and paint over the top. When it's dry, use a sharp pencil to add in the outlines.

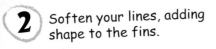

3 Shade the body and add the gills. Draw details inside the mouth.

The underside is pale.

4 Sharks have blue-gray backs and fins and pale underbellies. Shape the pale areas by adding areas of pale blue to shadowy places. Make the gums a pale pinky-red.

Bear

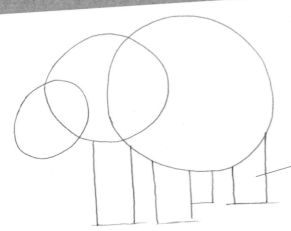

1 Draw two circles for the body. Add a smaller oval for the head.

Draw straight lines for the legs.

2 Shape the head, legs, and paws.

Add the ears.

The mouth is open.

Try drawing your bear on brown paper. The paper becomes the main body color to which you apply black and white to create shade and light.

3 Add more detail to the head. Begin to add the fur texture.

Add detail to the paws.

4 Shade in the eye and add the claws. Give shape to the body by adding extra detail to the fur.

5 Color using different shades of brown and black.

19

Dog

1 Draw a big, narrow oval for the body. Add a small circle for the head and two oblong shapes for the legs and tail.

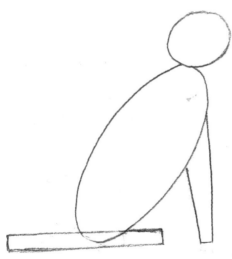

2 Shape the outline of the body.

Add the ears.

Make the lines for the tail wavy.

The back leg is bent, so add a curved line.

3 Erase the guidelines that you no longer need. Soften the outline to create a furry texture.

Now add the eyes, nose, and mouth.

Define the toes.

4 Add details to the nose, ears, and mouth. Continue to shade the fur.

Add markings by shading parts of the head.

The tail is extra fluffy.

5 Pressing gently, color your dog using lots of long lines in the direction of the fur. Add shading to the areas you have left pale with regular pencil or a brown shade.

Try working on textured paper. Use a soft pencil and color with gentle circular movements.

21

Parrot

1 Draw pointed shapes for the body, wings, and tail. Draw a circle for the head.

Add the curve of the beak.

2 Shape the beak and add a circle for the eye. Start to define the feathers on the wing and tail.

Lines for the perch.

Long lines for the tail feathers.

Try using watercolor pencils. Paint a little water over them to brighten the colors, and show details with a hard pencil.

Erase the guidelines and add detail to the eye.

The tip of the beak is the darkest area.

3 Shape the head and beak. Add shading to the feathers and features.

4 Color in sections, smudging some colors together. Use black for the beak and claws.

Lion

1 Draw a small oval with a larger circle around it for the head and mane. Draw a long oval for the body.

Add rectangular shapes for legs.

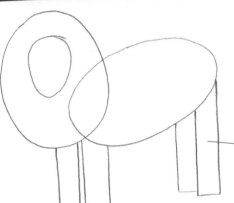

2 Add the features and the ears. Shape the legs.

Draw a guideline to help you place the features.

The tail is two curved lines.

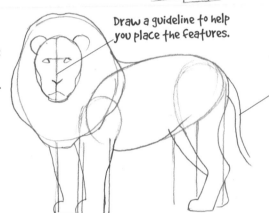

3 Erase the guidelines and add shading to the legs and belly.

Begin to shape the face.

Soften the outline of the mane.

finish the tail with lots of soft, short lines.

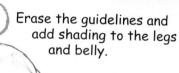

4 Make the mane look soft by adding lots of lines going outward from the head.

Add detail to the ears.

Add more shading to the legs that are farthest away.

5 Color using sandy browns in short, soft strokes. Leave highlights on the body. Add some dark orange shades to the head and mane.

Giraffe

1 Draw a triangle for the head. Draw a long shape for the neck, which should get wider as it joins the body.

The body is a squashed circle.

The legs are very thin triangles.

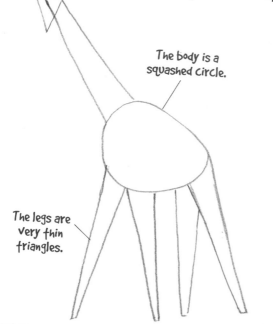

2 Begin to shape the head, neck, and legs. Add the eyes.

The horns are slimmer than the ears.

Add lines to show where the legs join the body.

Shape the hooves.

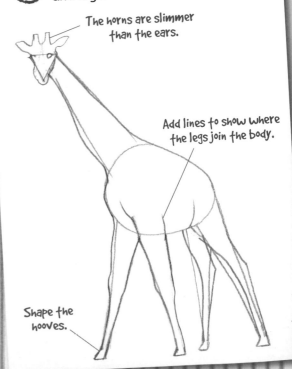

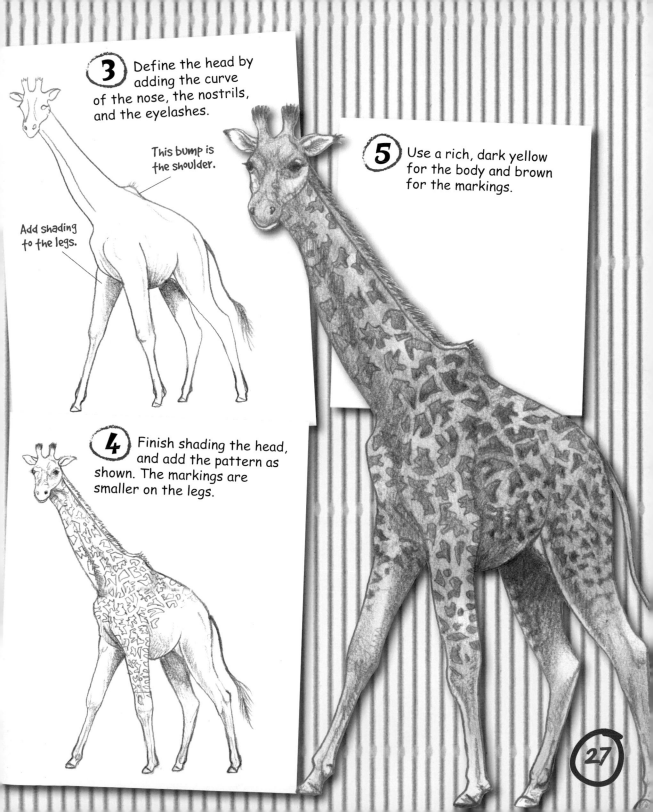

3 Define the head by adding the curve of the nose, the nostrils, and the eyelashes.

This bump is the shoulder.

Add shading to the legs.

5 Use a rich, dark yellow for the body and brown for the markings.

4 Finish shading the head, and add the pattern as shown. The markings are smaller on the legs.

Horse

1 Draw an oval for the body and triangles for the head, neck, and legs.

2 Begin to shape the head, neck, and body. Add the eye and ears.

Curve the line of the back.

3 Add the mane and flowing tail. Shape the hooves. Erase all the guidelines.

Add a line for the mouth.

Begin to add shading.

Try using a dull pencil to get an even color for the body. Then sharpen the pencil and use it to add fine lines of hair.

4 Deepen the shading and darken the lines of the horse's muscles.

Lines of muscle

Finish shading the legs.

5 Color the body a rich brown. Use a darker brown for the mane and tail.

cat

2 Draw circles for eyes and a triangle for the nose. The mouth is two lines. Add the tail.

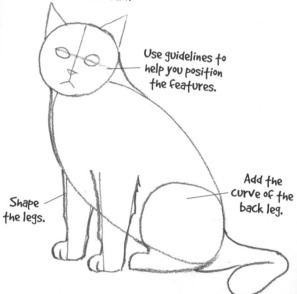

Use guidelines to help you position the features.

Add the curve of the back leg.

Shape the legs.

1 Draw a slanted oval for the body and a circle for a head. Add straight lines for the legs.

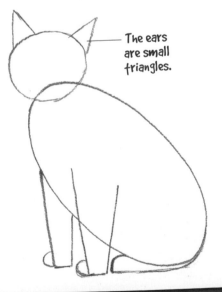

The ears are small triangles.

Try drawing fur on gray paper using a darker gray and white for highlights. Use black for stripes, and blend with the other colors.

3 Soften the outline and begin to add shading. Erase the guidelines.

Begin to add markings around the eyes.

4 Make the features more detailed. Continue to add texture to the fur.

Soften the head, adding lots of little lines.

5 Color using shades of gray in short lines, leaving patches on the chest and legs pale. Draw fine lines for the whiskers. Add stripes of different thickness in black. Color the eyes a deep orange or yellow.

READ MORE

Fraser, Mary Ann. *How Animal Babies Stay Safe*. Let's-Read-and-Find-Out Science. New York: HarperCollins Publishers, Inc., 2001.

Fujikawa, Gyo. *Baby Animal Families*. New York: Sterling Publishing, 2008.

Williams, Garth. *Baby Animals*. New York: Golden Books, 2004.

GLOSSARY

Highlights (HY-lytz) The palest areas where the light falls directly.

Perspective (per-SPEK-tiv) Point of view.

Shadow (SHA-doh) A dark spot made by a person or a thing that block the light.

Texture (TEKS-chur) How something feels when you touch it.

INDEX

C

Chalk pastels, 4, 11
Color, 4, 15, 29
Crayon, 5

F

Feathers, 8, 12–13, 22–23
Fur, 8, 19, 21, 31

H

Highlights, 4, 7, 25, 30

K

Kneaded eraser, 5, 7

P

Pen(s), 5

Pencil(s), 4–5, 7–8, 11, 15–16, 21, 23,

S

Stippling, 7

T

Tone, 6

WEB SITES

For Web resources related to the subject of this book, go to: www.windmillbooks.com/weblinks and select this book's title.